HOT TOPICS

FAIR TRADE

Jilly Hunt

www.raintreepublishers.co.uk
Visit our website to find out more information about Raintree books.

To order:
☎ Phone 0845 6044371
🖷 Fax +44 (0) 1865 312263
🖳 Email myorders@raintreepublishers.co.uk

Customers from outside the UK please telephone +44 1865 312262

Raintree is an imprint of Capstone Global Library Limited, a company incorporated in England and Wales having its registered office at 7 Pilgrim Street, London EC4V 6LB – Registered company number: 6695582

Text © Capstone Global Library Limited 2012
First published in hardback in 2012
The moral rights of the proprietor have been asserted.

Edited by Adam Miller, Nick Hunter, and
    Diyan Leake
Designed by Philippa Jenkins
Original illustrations © Capstone Global
    Library Ltd 2012
Picture research by Mica Brancic
Production by Eirian Griffiths and Alison Parsons
Originated by Capstone Global Library Ltd
Printed and bound in China by Leo Paper
    Products Ltd

ISBN 978 1 406 23503 6
15 14 13 12
10 9 8 7 6 5 4 3 2

British Library Cataloguing in Publication Data
Hunt, Jilly
Fair Trade – (Hot Topics)
382.3-dc22
A full catalogue record for this book is available from the British Library.

Acknowledgements
We would like to thank the following for permission to reproduce photographs: Alamy pp. 6 (© Picture Contact BV), 34 (© Joerg Boethling), 52 (© BrazilPhotos.com/Ricardo Funari); Corbis pp. 18 (© Image Source), 21 (© Michael S. Yamashita), 22 (Reuters/© Simon Newman), 37 (In Pictures/© Andy Aitchison), 39 (© Bojan Brecelj), 40 (© Pablo Corral Vega), 43 (epa/© Jon Hrusa), 45 (Reuters/© Mike Hutchings); Fairtrade org uk pp. 8 (© Marcus Lyons), 10; Getty Images p. 46 (AFP Photo/Issouf Sanogo); © Peter Caton pp. 17, 51; Photolibrary p. 12 (Lineair/Ron Giling); Rex Features p. 24 (Jason Alden), 36 (Robert Harding/Liba Taylor); © Simon Rawles pp. 4, 29, 30, 32, 36, 44, 48, 53, 55; Shutterstock pp. 16 (© Paul Prescott), 19 (© Arkadiusz Komski), 47 (© Ziggysofi).

Cover photograph of a farmer holding drying cacao beans at a fair trade co-operative in the Dominican Republic, 2007, reproduced with permission of Corbis (© Owen Franken).

Every effort has been made to contact copyright holders of material reproduced in this book. Any omissions will be rectified in subsequent printings if notice is given to the publishers.

CONTENTS

Some words are printed in bold, **like this**. You can find out what they mean by looking in the glossary.

WHAT IS FAIR TRADE?

In simple terms, "fair trade" is trade in which fair payment is made to the producers of the goods. **Consumers** pay a little bit extra to get a product that they know has been **ethically** produced. However, the concept of fair trade is a more complex issue which raises many questions. These include: "Who gets fair trade?", "Who decides what is fair payment?", "Why is fair trade needed?", "Shouldn't all trade be fair?", "Is fair trade good for everyone?", and "How do I know something is genuinely fair trade?" This book will help you explore these questions so you can decide for yourself what you think about this hot topic.

■ Fair trade has helped this farmer in the Windward Islands in the West Indies.

A bit more detail...

Fair trade is a social movement which aims to improve environmental and labour standards. It is concerned with the exports of raw material and goods from **developing countries** to **developed countries**. There are a number of organizations around the world that are involved with fair trade, and we will investigate some of these organizations in more detail throughout this book.

FINE is an umbrella organization of fair trade networks. It has provided the following definition:

> Fair trade is a trading partnership, based on dialogue, transparency and respect, which seeks greater equity [fairness] in international trade. It contributes to **sustainable development** by offering better trading conditions to, and securing the rights of, **marginalized** producers and workers – especially in the South. Fair trade organizations (backed by consumers) are engaged actively in supporting producers, awareness raising and in campaigning for changes in the rules and practice of conventional international trade.

This book will explore the benefits and disadvantages of fair trade, looking not only at the better trading conditions the movement offers, but also at the people left out of the scheme and what might happen to them.

What are fair trade products?

Fair trade supports producers in developing countries. Fair trade products are often raw materials such as coffee, cocoa, and bananas, or products made from these raw materials, grown in the developing countries. In the United States, fair trade certification is available for coffee, tea, herbs, cocoa, chocolate, fresh fruit, sugar, rice, and vanilla. In Europe, more products receive certification – even footballs can be fair trade certified!

Where are fair trade products sold?

Today you can find fair trade products in many shops, including supermarkets. There are even some towns called fair trade towns, where councils, schools, and shops use and promote fair trade. There are now over 750 fair trade towns around the world, including San Francisco, Rome, and London.

Why fair trade?

The farmers and producers involved with the fair trade scheme come from some of the poorest countries in the world. For them, **debt** can be a big problem. Fair trade can help them by offering a fair, stable price which will cover the cost of producing the goods. Fair trade can also help by improving access to no- or low-**interest** loans. This can make a big difference to a poor farmer. Other ways fair trade can help improve lives include:

- no enforced child labour
- safe, decent working conditions
- fair prices – farm groups receive a guaranteed minimum price and an additional premium for certified **organic** products
- help to gain skills and knowledge to develop their business
- more protection from the price decreases of the international **commodity** (raw material) market
- conservation of natural resources.

A fair trade farmer holds a packet of Max Havelaar coffee.

History of fair trade

The first fair trade label was launched in 1988. The label was called "Max Havelaar" after a character from a novel about the exploitation of coffee pickers in the Dutch colonies. The fair trade label was set up by a Dutch development agency called Solidaridad because the price of coffee worldwide began to fall quickly. The label gave the mainstream coffee industry the chance to work in a way that had not existed before.

Before this first fair trade label was set up, there were other initiatives called alternative trade organizations (ATOs). These were often started up by churches in North America and Europe to help refugees and other poverty-stricken communities after World War II by selling their handicrafts. The ATOs would buy the products from poor producers at an above-market price and sell them directly to consumers. ATOs continue to operate today and some are linked in with fair trade organizations. There are also companies who practise ethical trading. These companies try to ensure that the basic labour rights of employees of suppliers in developing countries are respected. The Ethical Trading Initiative is an alliance of companies, **trade unions**, and voluntary organizations whose aim is to protect and improve the working lives of people across the world in all stages of the supply chain.

FAIR TRADE AROUND THE WORLD

The fair trade model used with the "Max Havelaar" label was copied in markets across Europe and North America. "Max Havelaar" was used in Belgium, Switzerland, Denmark, Norway, and France. "TransFair" was used in Germany, Austria, Luxembourg, Italy, the United States, Canada, and Japan; "Fairtrade Mark", in the United Kingdom and Ireland; "Rattvisemarkt", in Sweden; and "Reilu Kauppa", in Finland.

What is the "fair trade model"?

The fair trade model works by organizing individual farmers into groups called **co-operatives**. These co-operatives may also be called the **producer organization**, which means they are the people who grow or produce the products. The advantage of forming a co-operative is that it is large enough to do business with the main buyers, such as supermarkets, who want to buy big quantities of a product. An individual farmer would not be able to produce enough to go directly to a main buyer. They would have to sell to a reseller. A reseller would buy from lots of individual farmers so that he or she would be able to gather enough produce to sell to a main buyer. However, the resellers would also need to make money, so they would not pay the individual farmer very much.

Supermarkets and other main buyers want to buy fair trade products so the co-operatives have to follow the fair trade standards for producing their products. These include ensuring working conditions are good and that the environment is cared for. In order to become fair trade, the co-operatives need to go through a series of checks which are done by an organization called **FLO-CERT**. If a co-operative meets the fair trade standards, they are allowed to use the fair trade label.

■ Look out for the fair trade label when you next go shopping.

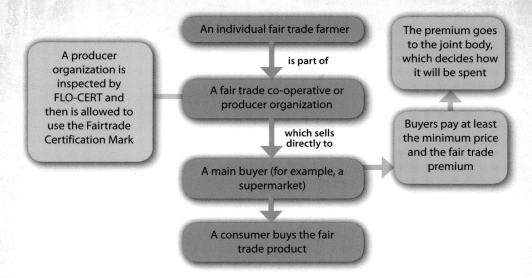

When buyers such as supermarkets buy a fair trade product, they must pay a minimum price for it. If the market price is higher than the minimum price, then the co-operative gets the market price. The buyer also has to pay a **fair trade premium**. This is a sum of money in addition to the price paid for the goods. The premium should be used on projects to improve the community, such as a new school, road, or water supply for the village. Within each co-operative there is a **joint body** that decides how this money should be spent. The joint body is a committee of people elected by the workers. It should include all types of workers, not just management.

WHO'S WHO IN FAIR TRADE?
- **Fairtrade Labelling Organizations International (FLO)** is responsible for setting fair trade standards and for use of the fair trade label.
- FLO-CERT is responsible for ensuring that the producer organizations are meeting fair trade standards.
- World Fair Trade Organization is the global representative body of over 400 fair trade organizations.
- A joint body is the committee responsible for ensuring the fair trade premium is used to benefit the community.
- A producer organization is a collection of farmers or workers.

How do I know something is definitely fair trade?

If you want to buy something that is guaranteed to be fair trade then you need to look out for the fair trade label. This is a guarantee that the product meets the fair trade standards. The Fairtrade Certification Mark or label is controlled by FLO. They control its use so the label cannot be used by just anyone. Any product with this label will have met the social, economic, and environmental standards set by fair trade. There are strict rules about using the mark but the mark only applies to products and not the company selling the product.

In 2002, FLO introduced the International Fairtrade Certification Mark to replace the individual labels used by fair trade organizations in different countries. This has made the labelling stronger and it is now the most widely recognized ethical label in the world. However, Canada and the United States are still using their original labels.

Fair trade certification

FLO-CERT runs the fair trade certification system. It inspects all the producers to ensure that the standards are met. It also checks that producers receive their minimum price and premium.

The International Fairtrade Certification Mark is based on the drawing of a human with an upraised arm. The idea is to present a positive message about fairness, empowerment, progress, and hope.

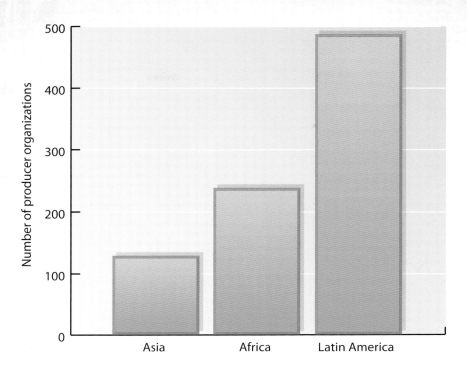

■ This graph shows how many producer organizations operate in Asia, Africa, and Latin America. These three continents are the main producers of fair trade goods, which are then consumed in places such as the United Kingdom, the United States, Australia, and other developed countries.

Making a difference

The story of Divine Chocolate is an interesting example of how fair trade, combined with some innovative thinking, can make a big difference to the lives it touches. Divine is the first fair trade chocolate bar to be aimed at the mass market in the United Kingdom. It was launched in the autumn of 1998 and is now sold in the United Kingdom, the United States, Canada, Sweden, Norway, and the Netherlands.

CASE STUDY

Divine Chocolate

In the early 1990s, the cocoa market in Ghana changed. Previously, the government controlled all of the cocoa buying in Ghana. This changed to allow private companies to become cocoa buyers. A number of farmers saw the opportunity to become cocoa buyers. They set up a farmers' co-operative, called Kuapa Kokoo, to sell their cocoa to the government-controlled Cocoa Marketing Company, which was the single exporter of cocoa from Ghana. As an organized company, they could make the selling process more efficient and ensure that its farmers got a fair price for their cocoa. In the past, farmers would use buying agents who often cheated farmers by using inaccurate weighing scales.

The co-operative started with just 200 members in 22 village societies and now has over 48,000 farmers in about 1,300 village societies. The co-operative was supported by a fair trade company called Twin Trading and by the Netherlands Development Organization.

■ The name of Kuapa Kokoo means "good cocoa farmer" in Twi, the local language. Their motto is *"pa pa paa"*, which means "best of the best of the best".

A bar of their own

At the 1997 annual general meeting (yearly meeting of members) of Kuapa Kokoo, members decided they would make their own chocolate bar. However, instead of aiming at the specialist, **niche market**, which many fair trade brands do, they would aim at the mainstream chocolate market. In 1998, Twin Trading, Kuapa Kokoo, and the Body Shop came together to set up a company called the Day Chocolate Company. The company also had support from Christian Aid and Comic Relief.

The Divine fair trade milk chocolate bar was launched in October 1998. By December 1998, it was on the supermarket shelves. An amazing success! The chocolate market in the United Kingdom alone is worth nearly £4 billion, and even a small share of this would prove beneficial to the cocoa farmers.

In 2006, the Body Shop made an even bigger difference to the co-operative by donating all its shares to them. Kuapa Kokoo now owns a 45 per cent share in the company and has two elected representatives on the board. In January 2007, the company changed its name to become Divine Chocolate Ltd and in February 2007, Divine Chocolate Inc. was launched in the United States.

Kuapa Kokoo's mission

The mission of the Kuapa Kokoo co-operative is to bring about:
- increased power and representation in the market for farmers
- social, economic, and political empowerment
- enhanced women's participation in all its affairs
- production processes that are economically efficient and non-polluting, and that conserve natural resources.

Kuapa Kokoo was a success, and more farmers wanted to join. The proportion of women farmers has risen from 13 per cent to nearly 30 per cent. It has a waiting list of villages wanting to join.

UNDERSTANDING WORLD TRADE

In order to fully understand how fair trade can make a difference, it is important to understand how world trade operates.

World trade can be very complicated, with different countries setting rules about how they want to trade with other countries. An organization called the **World Trade Organization (WTO)** deals with the rules of trade between nations around the world. The WTO is a forum for governments to negotiate trade agreements and to settle any disputes. Although it is the governments of countries that agree to the rules, the rules are there to help producers of goods and services, exporters, and importers to do business as freely as possible.

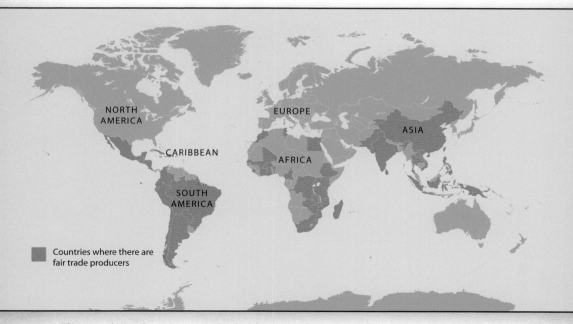

NORTH
AMERICA

EUROPE

ASIA

CARIBBEAN

AFRICA

SOUTH
AMERICA

Countries where there are fair trade producers

■ This map shows the countries in the Caribbean, South America, Africa, and Asia where there are fair trade producers.

CASE STUDY

Banana wars

In 1993, the WTO was called in to settle a trade dispute about bananas from the Windward Islands (Dominica, St Lucia, and St Vincent) having tariff-free entry to the **European Union** markets. Latin American and African producers were restricted by a system of quotas and tariffs. The WTO ruled that this was unfair and the Windward Islands' share of the UK banana market dropped from 40 per cent in 1992 to less than 9 per cent in 2009.

This caused real problems for the Windward Islands as the number of farmers decreased from 27,000 to 3,500. High unemployment caused an increase in poverty. Fair trade has helped banana farmers on the Windward Islands by providing the fair trade price and premium.

The rules might be different depending on what product or service is being traded but they all follow the same principles, which are:

- trade without discrimination – countries cannot have a preferred country to deal with and everyone should be treated equally.

- freer trade – using negotiation to lower trade barriers such as customs duties or **tariffs**, and import bans or quotas that restrict quantities selectively.

- predictability – ensuring that the rules remain constant means that businesses are better able to plan for the future.

- promoting fair competition – including applying rules about **dumping** (exporting at below cost to gain market share) and **subsidies** (money given by the state to help an industry).

- encouraging development and economic reform – in particular, in many **developing countries** which are in transition to market economies (where markets are free to trade without interference).

- protecting the environment – permitting members to take measures to protect not only the environment but also public health, animal health and plant health.

UNFAIR TRADE?

Having learned more about fair trade and world trade, perhaps you think that the world's standards for trade are OK. You may have the impression that there are systems in place to ensure a relatively fair trading environment.

However, while the **WTO** governs the rules of trade between nations, it does not cover the individuals involved in producing the goods or services. There are some people who simply want to make as much profit as they can, whatever the cost.

The cheapest supplier

It makes good business sense to look for the most cost-effective supplier for your business. Many companies in **developed countries** find they can get their goods and services by using companies in **developing countries**.

In the developing world, companies do not have to pay as much for an average wage. They also do not have to offer workers the same safety standards and protection. While this can provide employment in areas needing it, there are also companies who take advantage of the very poor population and pay very low wages.

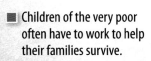 Children of the very poor often have to work to help their families survive.

■ Health and safety issues are often overlooked in the developing world.

Often, the poor are stuck in a poverty trap from which they cannot escape. They have poor living conditions and little or no education. They cannot afford to educate their children and may have to send them out to work. If the children do not get an education, it is almost impossible for them to improve their situation and break out of the poverty trap.

Some companies in the developing world pay little regard to working conditions. Employees often work in dangerous or unhealthy situations. The effects of their activities on the environment can also be neglected.

Big brand names

This kind of behaviour happens in many different industries, from mining and farming to clothing and electrical manufacturing. Very often it's not the big brand name companies who own the factories. These big name companies, such as Nike or Apple, are usually based in developed countries. They contract companies in developing countries to produce, for example, a new range of mobile phones for them. This company may then need to **subcontract** to other factories in order to produce as many phones as needed. The phone company may know very little about the conditions in the factories that are producing the goods for them.

Sportswear sector

As an example, let's look at the sportswear sector. Workers in this sector often face exploitative wages and conditions. Around 80 per cent of the hundreds of thousands of sportswear workers employed in Asia, Africa, Eastern Europe, and Latin America are women. Research by organizations including Oxfam International has found that sportswear workers work under high pressure for long hours, often in difficult and dangerous working conditions. Many face verbal and sexual harassment, their **trade union** rights are not respected, and their standard working week wages are too low to meet the most basic needs of their families. Some workers earn as little as €0.47 per hour – just €3.76 (£3.23) per day.

■ Do you think about what went into the production of your clothes and belongings? Who made this T-shirt and mobile phone? Under what conditions were they made?

Apple

It is not just in the sportswear sector where such practices are used. Apple, the computer and technology manufacturer, admitted in 2010 that at least eleven 15-year-old children had been discovered working in factories which supply Apple. It is not known which factories these children were working at but Apple works with factories in China, Taiwan, Singapore, the Philippines, Malaysia, Thailand, the Czech Republic, and the United States. Apple has previously been criticized for using factories where working conditions are poor. For example, in 2010, 62 workers in China were poisoned by a toxic chemical used at a factory that makes products for Apple and Nokia.

In 2009, a worker committed suicide after he was accused of stealing a prototype of the iPhone. He worked at a Taiwanese company that is one of Apple's biggest suppliers. An investigation into his death discovered that security staff from the factory had beaten him before he jumped to his death from the twelfth floor of his apartment block.

DEBATE

Is it the responsibility of all companies to ensure their suppliers are treating their workers fairly?

■ Many computers and their components are made in China.

CASE STUDIES

Nike

In 2001, the global sportswear giant Nike admitted that the company employed children in developing countries. There were reports that children as young as 10 were making shoes, clothing, and footballs in Pakistan and Cambodia for Nike.

Nike claimed that it had not ever intentionally employed children. Nike do not own the factories where these children were working and they did have age standards in place (18 years for footwear manufacturing, 16 years for clothing and equipment). But in some countries, such as Pakistan and Bangladesh, where records of birth do not exist or can be forged, it was hard to verify every employee's age. For example, in 1995 Nike had contracted what it thought were responsible factories in Sialkot, Pakistan to make footballs. The work was subcontracted and children were used in the production process.

Nike have put a new system of inspections in place to try to improve working conditions at their suppliers' factories. They have a team of 97 people who inspect several hundred factories a year. Nike also allows the Fair Labor Association (FLA) to do random inspections of their factories. The FLA was founded by human rights groups and companies such as Nike, Reebok, and Liz Claiborne.

A factory in Thailand

In November 2002, Lern, a factory worker in Thailand, gave an interview to Oxfam. She described the conditions she faced from 1998, when she started, to October 2002, when the factory closed. Lern described how she started work at 8.30 a.m. and most days she would work until 10 p.m. Three or four days a week, she would work until 2 a.m. During busy periods, such as Christmas, she would work through the night. She described how the factory owner would put drugs into some of the drink containers to

■ These employees are inspecting shoes in a shoe factory in China.

help them work through the night. Most workers took the drinks because it was the only way they could do the hours demanded of them. They would work up to 48 hours in a row before they collapsed from exhaustion.

Lern explained that they were told to lie to anyone visiting from Nike and say that they always finished work at 8 p.m. Before they had a visit from a Nike representative, they had to clean all the machines and were given cloth masks for the day. Workers would be stopped from admitting the truth to Nike representatives. The owner of the factory wanted to ensure that his employees did not form a **trade union**. He would make announcements over the loudspeaker warning workers who tried to form a union to "say goodbye to your parents". When the factory closed, the owner disappeared, owing payment to his workers.

FREE TRADE

Some people believe that there should be no trade barriers and that all countries should be allowed to trade freely. As things stand, there can be many obstacles which prevent **developing countries** from competing on a level playing field with **developed countries**.

CASE STUDY

Oxfam

Oxfam was first set up in 1942 as the Oxford Committee for Famine Relief. Its aim was to help Greek civilian victims of World War II and it continued from there. Oxfam opened its first shop in Oxford in 1948. This was one of the world's first charity shops.

■ Oxfam works in various ways to tackle poverty, including running their charity shops.

Is Oxfam International right to campaign about trade? Is it helping people in developing countries at the expense of those in developed countries?

Oxfam International

Oxfam International is an international confederation of fourteen organizations who work together in 98 countries to tackle poverty and injustice. It was set up in 1995, consisting of organizations which are based in Australia, Belgium, Canada, France, Germany, Great Britain, Hong Kong, Ireland, Mexico, the Netherlands, New Zealand, Quebec, Spain, and the United States. The aim of Oxfam International was to be a stronger force for change than fourteen organizations working independently. They work directly with communities and aim to influence the decision-makers to help poor people to improve their own lives.

Big noise, big success

One of Oxfam's ongoing campaigns concerns trade. Oxfam had a global campaign called "Make Trade Fair". They campaigned for decision-makers and governments to set up new trade rules. Their global petition for justice in trade, called "Big Noise", helped them lobby (put pressure on officials and law-makers) for change.

The "Big Noise" petition gathered over 20 million signatures. This helped Oxfam to lobby the **WTO**. Oxfam, together with other campaigning organizations and farmer groups, got the WTO to agree that by 2013, the rich, developed countries will have to stop subsidizing and **dumping** cheap exports on developing countries. Trade talks continue to take place at the WTO about a "development" trade deal that will help developing countries.

Campaigning for fair trade can be fun. At this event held in London in 2009, people were encouraged "do something silly for a serious cause", supporting farmers and co-operatives around the world.

The rules controlling trade have been set by the rich, **developed countries** and appear to favour them. For example, rich countries spend $1 billion a day **subsidizing** their farmers. These farmers produce too much and the extra is sold at vastly reduced prices. This sounds like a good thing, doesn't it – cheap produce for people who haven't got much money? The problem is that non-subsidized farmers cannot compete with the subsidized farmers, they cannot afford to sell their produce as cheaply, and therefore they cannot make a living. In many places, where farming is the only source of income, this pushes families even further into poverty.

For example, US cotton producers receive federal subsidies for each additional bushel of cotton they produce. This encourages US farmers to produce as much as they can, even if it is not needed. The extra, or surplus, is dumped on the international market. This makes international prices lower because there is so much of the product. Poor farmers cannot compete.

By reforming cotton subsidy, the welfare of over one million West African households – about 10 million people – could significantly improve as their incomes from cotton could increase by 8–20 per cent. In West Africa, cotton is often the only source of cash income for many families. Of course, the impact of such a change on US cotton farmers is another important issue to be considered.

Trade agreements can also make it difficult for poorer nations to compete. For example, the **European Union** protects its fruit farmers by imposing **tariffs** on imports from countries such as South Africa. These tariffs increase during peak European Union production and supply times. During the peak European Union summer production period, South African grapes have European Union tariffs of up to 14.1 per cent imposed on them. This makes South African grapes seem more expensive in comparison.

However, European Union producers are given tariff-free entry to South Africa. Because they do not have to pay expensive tariffs, European Union grapes can compete more favourably with locally grown South African grapes.

If Africa, Asia, and Latin America could increase their share of world exports by just one per cent, they would make enough money to help 128 million people get out of poverty. Oxfam International is an example of a **not-for-profit organization** that campaigns for improvements in trade to reduce poverty and injustice in the world.

FAIR PRICES AND A FAIR WAGE

Debt and **credit** are big issues for those struggling to get out of poverty. Debt is one of the biggest problems for farmers in **developing countries**. Often, the harvest does not bring enough money in to pay back the pre-harvest loans. The fair trade scheme can help farmer organizations by offering improved access to low- or no-**interest** loans. They also provide pre-harvest credit through buyers with whom they have long-term, stable contracts.

Fair trade also helps producers and workers to form their own democratic groups via **co-operatives** and workers' unions. As a co-operative, they are able to take advantage of the **economies of scale.** These bigger groups can negotiate better prices because they can supply larger quantities of the product. It also means that co-operatives can deal directly with the main buyer and do not have to go through agents who take a cut of the money.

■ These Indian rice farmers help produce one of the world's most consumed crops.

CASE STUDY

Sunstar Overseas and the Khaddar Farmers' Federation

Sunstar Overseas is an **organic** agribusiness (business involved in food production). It is one of India's largest rice exporters. Since 2001, it has worked in partnership with the Khaddar Farmers' Federation to develop organic farming on the flood plain in the Khaddar region in northern India. Sunstar provides good quality seeds, organic manures, and bio-pesticides at reduced rates and with interest-free credit. It has a contract with each farmer in the federation to buy their entire rice crop, but the farmers are not forced to sell exclusively to Sunstar.

Sunstar has identified fair trade as a means of improving the position of its farmers. The company is acting as a body that encourages the farmers to become a more coherent organization rather than the loose network they were before. In order to qualify for fair trade certification, the farmers must have a certain structure. There are now 23 village-level farmers' clubs, with a total of 520 rice farmers. By bringing the farmers together in this way, they will be in a stronger position to negotiate higher and more stable prices with buyers and to contribute to new resources for the communities.

Before fair trade involvement, these farmers would traditionally have to sell their rice to agents at a local market. The agents would pay very low rates, which often did not even cover the cost of producing the rice. Farmers would also find themselves having to borrow money from the agents at very high interest rates to pay for seeds and equipment.

The Khaddar Farmers' Federation have a proposed loan fund using their **fair trade premium**. A loan fund which charges low interest rates would mean that farmers could reduce their personal debts. It would also mean that the Federation's capital fund would grow through the interest payments.

Fair prices

The fair trade system is based on the **fair trade minimum price** and the fair trade premium. The fair trade minimum price is the lowest possible price a buyer, such as a supermarket or chocolate manufacturer, must pay the **producer organization**. If the market price is higher than the fair trade one, then the producers get the market price. The minimum price is set after consultation with fair trade producers and traders. It ensures that the producer is guaranteed to receive a price which covers the cost of sustainable production.

CASE STUDY

When fair trade connot help

Ambrose Martin Kimati is a coffee farmer. In 1998, the price of coffee began to fall to an all-time low. Ambrose cannot afford to fertilize his bushes or protect them from pests, so every year he gets less at harvest time. Although Ambrose is a member of a co-operative, his coffee is not of a good enough quality to be sold as fair trade. Ambrose cannot afford to improve the quality of his coffee without money in advance for fertilizers, so he cannot become a fair trade farmer.

The farmer will only get the fair trade price if there is a buyer willing to pay it. There is no guarantee about the quantity that will be sold at the fair trade minimum price. Many farmers sell a large proportion of their produce to the conventional market because there is more produce than the fair trade market wants. Some economists argue that fair trade encourages an oversupply of products that pushes prices down for other producers. Some people believe that farmers could gain more by specializing in a certain type of product. What do you think?

CASE STUDY

Fair trade price making a difference

A fair, stable wage helps families plan their finances and protects them from the rises and falls of market prices. Olive Kishero is a coffee grower in Uganda. Before the **co-operative** started buying their coffee, she and the other women would have to carry the coffee to market on their backs. This was sometimes as far as 10 kilometres (6 miles) away. When they got there, the traders would say that the coffee was no good and only offer them a low price. The women had little choice but to accept that. Olive says that fair trade is making a big difference to her.

■ The fair price Olive Kishero gets for her coffee helps her to pay the school fees for her children.

Fair trade premiums

The **fair trade premium** is paid as an addition to the minimum price. The premium is to be invested in developmental projects that are decided upon by the **joint body**, within each producer organization. There is a joint body on each farm. All types of workers are able to participate, and temporary and seasonal workers are included if they wish to be. Management staff are also included, so the workers can benefit from their expertise in areas such as project management.

The role of the joint body is to decide how best to use the fair trade premium to improve the lives of the workers, their families, and the community. It is not extra cash for individuals. According to **FLO**, in 2009, about $65 million was received by producers and their communities from the fair trade premiums.

■ This water pump was bought using fair trade premium. It provides safe, clean water for the village and has improved lives.

Premium improvements

Fair trade premiums have been used to improve lives within the community. For example, in Kenya, premiums received from selling fair trade flowers have been used:

- to help children who have been orphaned through **HIV/AIDS**

- for schooling for employees' children, as well as for employees themselves

- to drill bore holes to supply water to local villages

- to bring health facilities closer to the community

- to set up a mill so that subsidized maize is available to buy at 15 per cent below the market price for both workers and the wider community.

In Burkina Faso, Association Wouol produces organic mangoes and cashew nuts. They have used their fair trade premiums to:

- construct two bore holes for safe, clean water

- build a cereal bank. This is a building where rice and maize can be stored safely. When prices are low the rice and maize are kept here. It can then be sold when prices rise during the off season.

- fund teachers' salaries and contribute towards the running of a health centre.

WHO HELPS? ROOT CAPITAL

Root Capital is an example of a **not-for-profit organization** that helps provide finance for rural areas in developing countries (www.rootcapital.org). Root Capital is a social investment fund. This means that people can donate or invest money into the organization. It is from this pot of money that Root Capital can make loans to small businesses. Root Capital often uses future sales contracts from companies such as Starbucks and Marks & Spencer to ensure that those taking out the loan can pay it back. When the goods are sold, the small business pays Root Capital the interest and principal payment.

CASE STUDY

Small Organic Farmer Association

In Sri Lanka, members of the Small Organic Farmer Association (SOFA) are small-scale farmers who grow tea and spices. In partnership with a commercial company called Bio Foods, SOFA exports organic teas and spices. As its fair trade premium, SOFA buys 20 cows and 20 goats. These animals produce milk which can be sold to gain extra income. The cow dung is also important to their organic farming as it is used as fertilizer.

The premium has paid for new tea bushes to replace old ones. It has also been used to support women's programmes such as making reed baskets. These baskets are then used as packaging for up-market tea exports. The premium has allowed roads to be repaired and new ones to be built around the farms. This makes transport easier for the farmers and the whole community. SOFA has planned for the future. It sent 23 farmers on a tea farm management course. Thirty young farmers were trained in useful leadership and agricultural skills.

■ Tea-pickers can benefit from fair trade premiums.

How have most fair trade premiums been used?

Most producer organizations choose to spend half of their premiums on investing in their business. This includes training and buying equipment. It is sensible for producers to be investing their premiums in this way. It will help them to improve their products and increase how much they can produce. This will help ensure better success in the future.

There is a difference in the way worker groups spend their premiums. The worker groups are called hired labour organizations. These are groups of workers who work for somebody else (for example, as plantation workers). These people do not own the farms they work on but they still produce fair trade products, so they receive the fair trade premium. Because the workers do not own farms, the premium may not be spent on business development.

These groups tend to spend most of their premiums on supporting their local community and on projects that will improve career opportunities. These activities could include training, buying books and computers, and accessing the internet. A large amount of the premiums are often used for educational purposes.

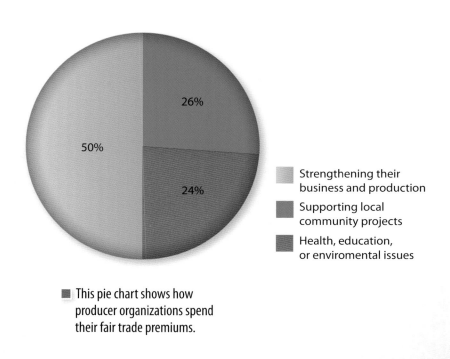

26%

50%

24%

Strengthening their
business and production

Supporting local
community projects

Health, education,
or enviromental issues

This pie chart shows how
producer organizations spend
their fair trade premiums.

Premium problems

What happens when the fair trade system of a fair price and a fair trade premium does not work? Research into fair trade shows that often very little of the premium paid for a fair trade product ends up with the producer. Some estimate that between 10 and 25 per cent goes to the producer. The rest is absorbed by the mark-up of wholesalers, importers, and retailers. Each of these people takes a cut of money to pay for the service they have provided.

Sometimes there is not enough premium to pass on to the farmers after paying operational costs. For example, in Guatemala, an executive at Federcocagua, the largest fair trade co-operative, admitted that after paying for the co-operative employees and programmes, there was nothing left for the farmers.

■ Some of the administration costs involved in being a member of the fair trade scheme cover the cost of employing inspectors. The inspectors play an important role in keeping the system operating fairly.

The way the premium is distributed to members through the joint body can allow for discrimination and unfair allocations of payments. Sarapi-Chok Chai Agriculture Cooperative Ltd in Thailand have an internal control system to help ensure the money is paid to the farmers. As well as five audits (official inspections) per year from government inspectors and the bank, each of the 103 villages that make up the co-operative selects their inspector to check the books.

Administration costs

Administration and fees for becoming a certified producer are expensive. The certification charge starts at £1,570 in the first year! The fair trade industry argues that having a proper system of checks and inspections in place is expensive. In addition, there needs to be a high cost on promotion because **consumers** have to be persuaded to spend the extra on a fair trade product. There are some farmers who cannot afford to be certified. However, FLO-International also offers small farmers' organizations the opportunity to apply for a grant to assist in paying for the fair trade certification.

Over to you

Think about the issues you've read about in this chapter. Does fair trade benefit the people it is trying to help? Is it leaving out the poorest of the poor, such as Ambrose on page 28? Could the benefits of fair trade be gained through normal business relationships? Is it distracting producers from finding speciality or **niche markets** where they could make more money? Is fair trade a "safe" way to help poor producers in **developing countries**?

Is it unfair for some people to have the benefit of fair trade status and not others?

LABOUR AND WORKING CONDITIONS

Probably one of the most appealing features of a fair trade product to a **consumer** is the promise that no enforced child or slave labour has been involved in the making of the product. This is in contrast to some of the factories discussed on pages 20–21.

No enforced child labour

Sadly, despite there being laws to protect children, enforced child labour happens in many countries all over the world. From farming to clothes manufacturing to mining, there are examples of children being forced into work.

In Burkina Faso, 12-year-old Ouare Fatao Kwakou was sold by his uncle to work as a cocoa picker in Ghana. Ouare had not received any payment for his labour. All the money went to his new owners and to the uncle who sold him.

■ These children in Somalia are preparing fields for the next season's maize crop.

■ Kuapa Kokoo are now working with the International Labour Organization to try to find ways to combat child labour.

According to the **United Nations**, 126 million children are occupied in the worst forms of labour such as in mines, with chemicals and pesticides in agriculture, or with dangerous machinery. Fifty million of these children work in Africa, in countries south of the Sahara Desert.

What about fair trade producers?

Even with fair trade certified products, it is hard to guarantee that no children have been involved. For example, the **co-operative** Kuapa Kokoo seems to be a fair trade success story. It is made up of 1,200 different cocoa societies that together are made up of 45,000 farmers. Kuapa Kokoo owns 45 per cent of Divine Chocolate Ltd and 33 per cent of Divine Chocolate USA, Inc. It also supplies fair trade chocolate to Cadbury. However, in September 2009, Kuapa Kokoo suspended 7 out of 33 of their cocoa farming communities after they were found to be using the worst forms of child labour. The director of the Fairtrade Foundation in the United Kingdom said that the fact that the communities were suspended shows that the fair trade system is working. What do you think?

Can child labour ever be right?

In many **developing countries**, children have traditionally been involved in the family business or farm. They are often there from a very young age, strapped to their mother's back as she harvests the crop. It is a way of life for many children in rural areas in developing countries to help out on the family farm. From about 4 years of age, children will be in the field, helping with weeding and picking for about 3 or 4 hours a day. They help feed the family's animals such as the chickens and cows, and they will also help out with the cooking and cleaning.

There is an argument that if a child is working on a family farm, he is being looked after by the family group and is thus given tasks that are appropriate for his skills and age. In some cases, it is the child's contribution to the family income that allows the family to pay for their child to attend school.

In addition, in some areas in countries such as Ghana, schools require their pupils to do farm work at least once a week. This is so the school can raise money by producing crops. Children are made to do hard manual work using machetes (sharp, heavy knives). This farm work for the school is more dangerous for the children because they are not as closely supervised as at home. They are also working near to each other so clearing land with machetes could result in injury. Many children prefer to stay at home to help on the family farm.

MAKING A DIFFERENCE: FREE THE CHILDREN

Free the Children was founded by a schoolboy and his classmates in 1995. It is now the world's largest network of children helping other children through education. It works in 45 countries and has over one million young people involved with it (www.freethechildren.com).

What is the fair trade stance on child labour?

Fair trade recognizes that many children are required to work to overcome their own or their family's poverty. Fair trade distinguishes between working children and child labourers.

■ A mother with her baby strapped to her back harvests crops in Zimbabwe.

Fair trade defines *child work* as work that still allows a child to attend school and that is not dangerous for them. It defines *child labour* as work that is hazardous, is exploitive or undermines a child's education or their emotional or physical health, such as being removed from their families and living in slave-like conditions. A ban on child labour by fair trade could make very poor families worse off or it may force children into more dangerous occupations.

Fair trade sees its work as protecting children by not allowing enforced child labour. But also, by providing fair payment for their families' produce, the family income is increased and so the hope is that the family will rely less on the work of their children.

DEBATE

Should all children be banned from working or is it acceptable for children to work if their family is very poor?

Safe working conditions

What do we mean by safe working conditions? We mean that:

- employment is entered into freely – there is no slavery or bonded labour (where workers only receive accommodation and food)

- employees have freedom of association – workers are allowed to join **trade unions** without the risk of losing their jobs

- the working environment is safe and hygienic – every day 6,000 people around the world die from work-related accidents or diseases

- enforced child labour is not permitted

- wages paid are enough to live on

- working hours are not excessive – they should not be over 48 hours per week

- discrimination does not occur – women and minorities are often denied promotions or training and so are stuck in the lowest paid jobs

- workers are not subjected to physical, verbal, or sexual abuse.

■ These workers at a plantation in Ecuador wear masks as they prepare to cut roses.

Trade unions

Trade unions can have a big impact on the quality of workers' lives. A trade union is an organization of workers who have joined together in order to achieve common goals, such as improving working conditions. By working together, unions are more powerful at negotiating with the management of a company on issues such as pay, working hours, benefits, complaints procedures, and workplace safety. The power a union can hold means that some companies do not want to allow unions to exist. You may remember that Lern's factory owner threatened violence against the parents of employees who tried to join a union (see page 21).

In many ways, being involved in the fair trade scheme has similar benefits to a trade union. Small-scale farmers can group together to form a co-operative which can then influence the big buyers.

International standards

There are international standards for safe working conditions. Some countries may have their own regulations. So what advantage does fair trade have? Well, as we have seen there are companies prepared to ignore international standards and regulations to gain maximum profit. Fair trade has the benefit of active inspections and enforcement.

Many of the flowers you might see for sale come from farms in **developing countries**, such as Ecuador or Kenya. Patricia Torres, a flower worker in Ecuador, explains that when she became pregnant while working at a previous flower farm she had to continue to do heavy work. She and her baby were exposed to pesticides because the farm would fumigate (treat with fumes to kill germs and pests) the flowers while the workers were still in the greenhouse. In her current job, everything is different. Pregnant women do not do the heavy work and are allowed to go home at 2.30 p.m.

EMPOWERING PEOPLE AND EDUCATION

Fair trade works in many ways to help people feel empowered. This means that they feel that they have control over their own lives. By helping to establish the **co-operatives** people are given organizational and business skills that they can use in other areas of their lives to improve their incomes. Fair trade can also give people confidence and self-esteem. This gives them the ability to deal successfully with big international companies and to take control of their own lives.

Meeting challenges

In Kenya, in January and February 2008, there were riots linked to charges of vote rigging in the general election. The country was in turmoil. People were forced to leave their homes. The unrest hit Kenya's major foreign currency earners, which are tea, flowers, and tourism. No one wanted to holiday in a country in the middle of a riot. Exporting tea and flowers was incredibly difficult because the riots disrupted the roads and power supplies.

February and March are busy times for the Kenyan flower industry. They had orders from around the world for Valentine's Day and Mother's Day. Workers knew that it was essential to carry on so that, once the riots were over, the businesses could return to normal, and people could continue to earn an income from them. Because they felt involved in the business, the workers and management struggled to keep everything running as normally as possible. They put in enormous efforts to ensure that orders were met. Some fair trade certified farms used their premium money to help those workers who had had to flee their homes.

The rioting in Kenya in 2008 threatened to disrupt the country's economy.

End of apartheid

Apartheid is the name given to the white South African government's system of racial segregation which began in 1948. The segregation policy discriminated against South Africa's non-white population and prevented black people from owning property. When apartheid ended in 1994, all South Africans had equal rights in law. However, because of apartheid, the black population was severely disadvantaged. For example, about 40 per cent of the black population were unemployed whereas just 5 per cent of whites were unemployed.

The white minority also owned 85 per cent of agricultural land. The new South African government introduced a land reform programme to redistribute land to tackle poverty and inequality. The programme's aim is to increase black ownership of agricultural land to 30 per cent by 2015.

Empowerment farms

Fair trade has been used in conjunction with empowerment farms to help disadvantaged farmers in South Africa. Empowerment farms are joint enterprises with white owners of large commercial farms, where black farm workers form a trust to buy a 25–50 per cent share in the farming company. The trust members elect representatives who are involved in strategic decisions, such as approving the budget. Alternatively, the workers' trust could buy a plot of land to establish their own farm. What makes the empowerment farms in South Africa successful is the involvement of the white co-owners who have the agricultural and commercial experience.

Empowering women

The tradition in many of the communities in **developing countries** is for the women to manage the house and help with the farming. It is a male-dominated society. If a husband says a wife can't go out to work, then she must stay at home. Fair trade is helping to give women more independence.

"Fairtrade is ... giving women freedom of speech. When we are paid we buy what we want and don't have to ask our husbands, and we know how to budget for our household needs."

Jennipher Wattaka (shown here)

■ These workers are harvesting grapes at Bouwland wine farm in South Africa. In 2004, labourers bought a 74 per cent share of this empowerment farm.

CASE STUDY

Keboes Fruit Farm

When Karsten Fruit Farms in South Africa wanted to expand, it decided this was a good opportunity to increase the economic empowerment of its farm workers. A group of 300 workers set up a trust to buy a 23 per cent share in the new company, which is called Keboes Fruit Farm. The workers' shares will be held in a trust operated by the government's Industrial Development Corporation for 10 years. During this time, the workers must pay for their shares, either through government grants or through dividends (payments that they will receive as shareholders).

Changing lives

Fair trade sales and premiums have changed women's lives. It has provided opportunities for women to earn their own income and gain some independence. It has also provided funds to help with health care, alternative income opportunities, small loans, education, and leadership training. For example, the Cecocafeen **co-operative** in Nicaragua used their fair trade premiums to offer small business loans for women, build a health centre, and provide finance for health services.

In Burkina Faso, the Union of Women Producers of Shea Products of Sissili and Ziro are using their premium funds to extend the literacy programme and for the long-term funding of a children's day care and playground project. Most of the women involved in shea butter production are illiterate, so being able to continue with the literacy programme will benefit many. The daycare centre will help give women the time to work.

■ These women from a co-operative are preparing shea butter. Sales of soap and cosmetics containing this ingredient are helping African women feed their children and send them to school.

Fair trade also provides opportunities for women to take a leadership role in the co-operatives. The premiums can be used to give women opportunities to generate income in other ways. For example, women can gain an additional income using sewing machines bought using fair trade premiums.

■ Sewing machines are used to generate more income.

CASE STUDY

Café Femenino

Café Femenino was set up as a women-only sub-group of a coffee co-operative in Peru. It now has 5,000 women growers from eight countries. The coffee these women grow is sold under the "Café Femenino" brand. The coffee buyers are required to donate a portion of the proceeds from the coffee sales to a local domestic violence organization or to the Café Femenino Foundation. The Café Femenino fair trade premiums have been used to provide:

- leadership and management training
- crop diversification programmes so that people are not reliant on the success of just one crop
- a permanent medical post.

The premiums have even been used for home improvements so that the women can have simple raised indoor kitchens. Before this, women would have to bend over an open fire on the ground. Many would suffer chronic back pain and health issues connected with breathing in the "kitchen" smoke.

Fair trade and education

What does it feel like to be able to read this book? What about reading your favourite magazine, emails from friends, or even just the flavour on a can of drink? Well, around 799 million people over the age of 15 years could not read any of these things. Many children in developing countries start life without adequate food, let alone an education. Many families cannot afford to send their children to school. Even if schooling is free, they cannot afford the expense of books and equipment. If a family do find some funds for schooling then it is traditionally the boys who are educated. That is why over 500 million of the world's illiterate adults are women.

According to the United Nations Children's Fund (UNICEF), there are just 96 girls for every 100 boys in primary school around the world, and the difference is greater at secondary level. An uneducated woman is at a big disadvantage. Not only is she more likely to contract **HIV/AIDS** than an educated woman, but she will be less likely to be able to support herself, with only very low paid work available to her. She will have a low bargaining position in the household and community, and will be less able to take advantage of her legal rights. These problems will also affect her children. She will be less likely to get her children vaccinated against illnesses and to know how to help them survive.

■ This school in the Windward islands is funded by fair trade premiums.

"When I was young, I didn't have the opportunity to study, and for that reason I give thanks to Fairtrade because it has enabled me to pay for my studies as an adult. I now have an undergraduate degree in sustainable agriculture. I am educating my children as I would have liked to have been educated at their age."

Blanca Rosa Molina, a member of a coffee co-operative in Nicaragua

MAKING A DIFFERENCE: UNICEF

UNICEF is an international organization that focuses on the protection of children's right to a basic quality of life. They are in the unique position of having the authority to influence decision-makers around the world. One of UNICEF's goals is to promote girls' education because it benefits all children. Educated girls become better parents to their own children, as well as better thinkers and better citizens.

It is not surprising, then, that many communities decide to spend their **fair trade premiums** on education, and especially on improving access to education for girls. For example, the Dougourakoroni Cotton Producers Co-operative in Mali spent their first fair trade premiums on building one school and a block of three classrooms for the village. Before this, the children were taught outside so lessons were cancelled during bad weather. The premiums have also been used to fund literacy programmes and provide training in specific skills.

Should all children have the right to an education?

NATURAL RESOURCES AND THE ENVIRONMENT

For a product to be called fair trade, it must be produced in an environmentally responsible way. But who decides what is "environmentally responsible"? FLO is a member of the ISEAL Alliance, which is a global association for social and environmental standards. ISEAL work with companies, **not-for-profit organizations**, and governments. They set codes of good practice. These are models of good ways of working for organizations to follow. These codes let **consumers** know what products and services have been **ethically** sourced and help the environment. They guarantee producers a living income.

CASE STUDY

Agrocel Pure and Fair Cotton Grower's Association

Agrocel Pure & Fair Cotton Grower's Association in India are working with Agrocel Industries to convert to organic farming. Cotton farmers are facing tough challenges with the price of cotton being unstable and in decline due to United States and **European Union dumping** of cheap cotton. Agrocel have seen an opportunity to access a **niche market**. By converting to organic farming, the farmers are improving their environment as well as being paid more for it. The cotton industry uses high quantities of chemical pesticides. These harm the environment and those communities living within it. The traditional method of irrigation by flooding is making water a scarce **commodity**.

Fair trade's environmental standards

There are fair trade rules about the use of chemicals, disposal of waste, and protection of natural resources. They also prohibit the use of **genetically modified organisms** (**GMOs**, in which the genetic material in cells are altered). Where it is practical, they encourage **organic** farming. Fair trade producers are expected to minimize the use of chemical fertilizers and insecticides and instead begin to use natural fertilizers and biological methods of disease control (for example, introducing a natural predator of the pest rather than using chemicals).

Does the fair trade label mean that a product is also organic?

No. Fair trade encourages organic farming, but the label does not certify this. Many fair trade groups do use their **fair trade premiums** to train producers in organic techniques such as composting. Producers of some products have converted to organic farming practices because they can make more money this way.

OVER TO YOU

Is it right that fair trade prohibits the use of GMOs? Using a genetically modified crop might help produce more harvest or protect the crop from being attacked by pests. What do you think? FLO states that many consumers are concerned about GMO crops and the risk to the environment, but also that the producers will become dependent on GMO seed.

CASE STUDY

How the Brazil nut can protect the Amazon rainforest

Did you know that Brazil nuts, or Amazon nuts as they are known locally, only grow in a specific area of the Amazon rainforest? The trees grow in an area covered by Bolivia, Brazil, and Peru. The trees can live for up to 1,000 years! Each tree grows up to 1,300 pods, which are each the size of a grapefruit. These pods contain about 20–40 Brazil nuts. During the rainy season, from January to March, the pods drop to the floor and are collected by nut gatherers. The nut gatherers fill bags weighing up to 70 kilograms (155 pounds) – that's the weight of an adult man! The bags are carried through narrow forest tracks or by boat to shelling and drying factories.

The Brazil nut is protecting the environment by providing an income for local people living in the area. This is especially important because the decline in the price of rubber, which is the main source of income in this area, has meant that areas of the Amazon are being cleared for cattle grazing or growing soya. By providing a source of income that doesn't involve cutting down trees, the Brazil nut helps to preserve the rainforest. However, as with most agricultural products, the price of Brazil nuts can fluctuate, too, so fair trade can help provide a more stable income.

■ These workers are loading Brazil nuts for export.

Not a cheap treat

In the chocolate industry, there are predictions that in years to come there will be no more cheap chocolate. This is because of the time-consuming work that it takes to maintain cocoa plants and the little rewards farmers receive for their efforts (50 pence a day). As their trees die off, farmers need to move to a new area of forest to replant. They then have to wait 3 to 5 years for the new plants to mature. Farmers also have to cope with pest problems. In addition, cocoa is competing for space with palm oil, which is in great demand for biofuels (fuel made from plant matter). The younger generation of African farmers is moving to the cities for work rather than do such difficult work for so little pay. Some farmers in West Africa have turned to child labour to make up for lack of adults willing to do the work. This is where fair trade can benefit. The next generation of farmers could be encouraged to stay if they see that they can receive a better price for the cocoa.

■ This farmer from Ghana is cutting cocoa pods from a tree.

MAKING A DIFFERENCE: EARTHWATCH

Earthwatch (www.earthwatch.org) is a not-for-profit organization working around the world. It has been working in partnership with Cadbury Schweppes to investigate cocoa production in Ghana. The project team will encourage new farming techniques and aim to get farming going again on land where cocoa was once grown. They will also test the concept of eco-tourism to take advantage of the millions of visitors to Ghana.

CONCLUSION

So, what do you think about fair trade? Is it a good thing? Is it a restrictive thing because some people are excluded from the benefits of joining a fair trade scheme? Is it better to help some people rather than help no one? Should people be focusing on improving world trade in general?

We've seen examples of when fair trade works, such as for the Kuapa Kokoo cocoa **co-operatives** in Ghana with their Divine Chocolate bar. But we've also read about people who are desperate because fair trade is not helping, such as Ambrose, the coffee farmer in Tanzania. We've investigated how world trade works and seen how it can work to benefit some but at the expense of others, such as during the banana wars of the Windward Islands. We've seen how rich nations still seem to have the advantage. For example, the **dumping** of subsidized cotton from the **European Union** and United States on to the world market forces down prices to an unstable level for those farmers in **developing countries**. We've explored what happens when the welfare of people is neglected in order for people in the West to get the latest mobile phone or pair of trainers.

What about the organizations involved in helping developing countries out of poverty? Charities and **not-for-profit organization**s, such as Oxfam International, can make a big difference. Is the fair trade scheme needed as well? What do you think? Is it good that there are many different ways in which people are trying to help improve the lives of the very poor in developing countries? Or should everyone try to make one scheme work?

What about the lives of farmers in the **developed countries**? What will happen to the cotton farmers in the European Union and United States when subsidies are stopped? Should we be making it our priority to buy local produce and support those around us?

DEBATE

Should all trade be fair trade or should trade be made fair?

■ Fair trade works for some farmers, such as this olive grower in the West Bank.

DEBATING AND RESEARCH TOOLS

Fair trade summary

- What are fair trade products?

  Fair trade products originate from **developing countries** and include bananas, cocoa, coffee, dried fruit, fresh fruit and vegetables, honey, juices, nuts, oil seeds, oil, quinoa, rice, spices, sugar, tea, wine, beauty products, cotton, cut flowers, ornamental plants, and sports balls.

- What organization certifies fair trade products?

  The Fairtrade Certification Mark is a registered trademark of **FLO** and it is used by the fair trade organizations around the world. The fair trade producers and their products are certified by **FLO-CERT**.

- Who checks that producers are following the fair trade standards?

  FLO-CERT has a team of auditors (accounts inspectors) who make regular checks on the producers to ensure the fair trade standards are maintained.

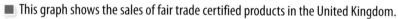

This graph shows the sales of fair trade certified products in the United Kingdom.

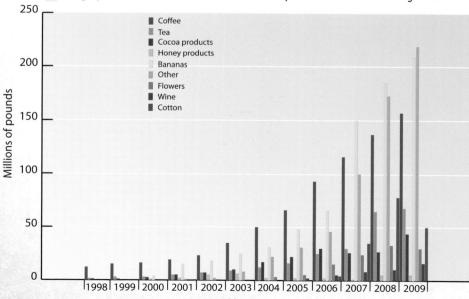

Timeline

Date	Event
Late 1980s/ early 1990s	"Max Havelaar" label is established and the initiative is copied across Europe and North America
1991	Oxfam helps set up a fair trade coffee company called Cafédirect
1992	Fairtrade Foundation in the UK is set up with the help of Oxfam
1993	Kuapa Kokoo **co-operative** is set up
1995	Oxfam International is set up Free the Children is founded by a schoolboy and his classmates
1997	Fairtrade Labelling Organizations International (FLO) is established to combine all initiatives and establish global standards and certification
1998	Fairtrade USA begins trading
1998	The Divine fair trade chocolate bar is launched
2001	Nike admits that the company employed children in developing countries
2002	FLO brings in the international fair trade certification mark to improve the visibility of the mark on shop shelves, and to make it easier to export products for the producers and the exporters
2003	The fair trade label is introduced to Australia and New Zealand
2004	FLO becomes two independent organizations: FLO, which sets fair trade standards and supports producers, and FLO-CERT, which inspects and certifies producers and audits traders. Café Femenino Foundation is set up
2006	The three different labelling initiatives – TransFair USA, TransFair Canada and Max Havelaar Switzerland – begin to adopt the new International Fairtrade Certification Mark
2007	Twenty-one labelling Initiatives are members of FLO International. Mexico, Australia, and New Zealand are new members Worldwide sales have increased by 47 per cent
2009	The World Trade Organization rules that the Windward Islands had an unfair trade agreement with the **European Union** for bananas
2010	There are now 24 organizations involved with FLO International Apple admits that at least eleven 15-year-olds had been discovered working in factories that supply it
2011	Cafédirect becomes the sixth largest coffee brand in the UK
2013	Rich, **developed countries** have to stop subsidizing and **dumping** cheap exports on the world market

What are the disadvantages of fair trade?

- There is no guarantee about the quantity that will be sold at the fairtrade minimum price. Many farmers sell a large proportion of their produce to the conventional market because there is more produce than the fair trade market wants.
- Some economists argue that fair trade encourages an oversupply of products that pushes prices down in general for other producers.
- Some people believe that farmers could gain more by growing speciality brands of their products.
- Often very little of the **fair trade premium** ends up with the producer.

What about buying local and supporting local farmers?

- Fair trade may divert the attention of poor countries from developing their own international labels.
- It is not clear that fair trade benefits the poorest producers (as shown by Ambrose's story).
- There are high administration fees involved in becoming a certified producer.
- Some believe the benefits of fair trade can be found through normal business relationships.

Countries with fair trade producers

Africa – Benin, Burkina Faso, Cameroon, Comoros Islands, Ivory Coast, Democratic Republic of Congo, Egypt, Ethiopia, Ghana, Kenya, Madagascar, Malawi, Mali, Mauritius, Morocco, Mozambique, Palestine, Rwanda, Senegal, Sierra Leone, South Africa, Swaziland, Tanzania, Togo, Tunisia, Uganda, Zambia, Zimbabwe

Asia – China, India, Indonesia, Kyrgyzstan, Laos, Pakistan, Papua New Guinea, Philippines, Sri Lanka, Thailand, Timor-Leste, Vietnam

Latin America and the Caribbean – Argentina, Belize, Bolivia, Brazil, Chile, Colombia, Costa Rica, Cuba, Dominican Republic, Ecuador, El Salvador, Guatemala, Haiti, Honduras, Jamaica, Mexico, Nicaragua, Paraguay, Peru, Windward Islands

Debating topics

- Fair trade is good. It is better to help some people than to help no one.
- Fair trade encourages the overproduction of some goods.
- Child labour is not acceptable in any situation.
- The environment should be protected at all costs.

Further research

Here are some other charities which you could research.

- International Save the Children
- VillageReach
- Stop the Traffik
- Feed the Children

FLO Statistics

- There are 827 fair trade certified **producer organizations** in 58 countries, representing over 1.2 million farmers and workers.
- In 2008, approximately €43 million was used in community development
- FLO estimates that six million people directly benefit from fair trade including families and dependents
- Between 2008 and 2009, sales of fair trade certified products grew by 15 per cent
- In 2008, fair trade certified sales was approximately €3.4 billion worldwide.

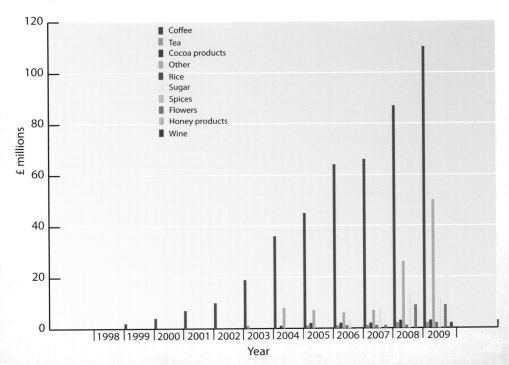

■ This graph shows the sales of fair trade certified products imported into the United States.

GLOSSARY

AIDS acquired immune deficiency syndrome, a disease which causes the breakdown of the human immune system and so leaves the body open to attack by infectious diseases

co-operative group of people who work together

commodity raw material or agricultural product that can be bought and sold

consumer person who buys goods and services. When you buy something from a shop, you are a consumer.

credit practice of allowing a buyer to receive goods or services in return for a promise to pay at a later date

debt something owed, such as money

developed country country in which the income is high enough to ensure that most people have a high level of well-being

developing country country in which the income is not yet high enough to ensure that most people have a high level of well-being

dumping sale of goods abroad at prices below their market value

economy of scale decrease in cost of a product resulting from buying in larger quantities

ethical fair, or morally correct

European Union organization of 27 European countries that decides on economic, social, and security policies that they have in common

fair trade minimum price lowest possible price a buyer must pay a producer organization

fair trade premium sum of money paid in addition to the price paid for goods. The premium should be used on projects to improve the community.

Fairtrade Labelling Organizations International (FLO) organization responsible for setting fair trade standards and for use of the fair trade label

FLO-CERT organization responsible for ensuring that producer organizations are meeting fair trade standards

genetically modified organism (GMO) organism changed by scientists in such as way that it passes particular features on to the next generation

HIV human immunodeficiency virus; virus which attacks the capacity of the body to defend itself against infection

interest fee charged for the use of credit or borrowed money

joint body committee of people democratically elected by the workers of a producer organization. The joint body decides how the fair trade premium should be spent.

marginalize keep a person or group away from influence or power

niche market small group of consumers that is interested in buying special products

not-for-profit organization organization that uses the money it earns or raises to run that organization and do its work. It may also be called a non-profit or non-profit-making organization.

organic develop naturally. Organic food is produced without using any chemicals.

producer organization group of people who grow or produce fair trade products

subcontract contract to supply some of the goods or services necessary to carry out a prior contract made with someone else

subsidy money given by the state to help an industry

sustainable development process of social and economic development that meets the needs of the present without compromising the ability of future generations to meet their own needs. Sustainable development involves minimal impact on the environment.

tariff government tax on goods that come into a country

trade union organization of workers who join together to achieve common goals, such as improving working conditions

United Nations (UN) international organization of countries to promote international peace, security, and co-operation

World Trade Organization (WTO) forum for governments to negotiate trade agreements and to settle any disputes

FURTHER INFORMATION

Books

50 Reasons to Buy Fair Trade, Miles Litvinoff and John Madeley (Pluto Press, 2007)

Fair Trade? (World Issues), Adrian Cooper (Franklin Watts, 2008)

The Fairtrade Everyday Cookbook, Sophie Grigson (editor) (Dorling Kindersley, 2010)

Is That Fair? Fair Trade (Worldscapes), Mary Atkinson (Heinemann Library, 2009)

Articles and reports

"Chocolate: worth its weight in gold?", *The Independent*, Monday 8 November 2010, independent.co.uk/life-style/food-and-drink/features/chocolate-worth-its-weight-in-gold-2127874.html

Offside! Labour rights and sportswear production in Asia, Tim Connor and Kelly Dent (Oxfam International, 2006, oxfam.org.au/resources/filestore/originals/OAus-OffsideLabourRightsAsia-1206.pdf)

"Tracing the bitter truth of chocolate and child labour", *Panorama*, BBC, Wednesday 24 March 2010, news.bbc.co.uk/panorama/hi/front_page/newsid_8583000/8583499.stm

Websites

Discover more about fair trade and its associations at the following websites:

Fairtrade Association for Australia and New Zealand **www.fta.org.au**

Fair Trade USA **www.transfairusa.org**

Fairtrade Foundation UK **www.fairtrade.org.uk**

Fairtrade Labelling Organizations International **www.fairtrade.net/home.html**

Find out more about Divine Chocolate at **www.divinechocolate.com/default. aspx**

Read more about Oxfam's campaigns and work at **www.oxfam.org**

Topics for further research

- Investigate apartheid in South Africa and learn more about why the current government are encouraging land redistribution.

- Research more about ethical trading and how it differs from fair trade.

- Investigate the employment practices of big multinational companies and learn more about their policies for employee welfare in their supplier factories.

INDEX